Steam on West of England Main Lines

Peter W. Gray

Front Cover: Towards the end of a busy summer Saturday, 4-6-0 No 7024 *Powis Castle* drifts alongside the River Exe towards Dawlish Warren with the 1.20pm from Paddington to Kingswear on 29 July 1961.

Rear Cover: Evening at Kingswear on 30 August 1961. The *Alfred Everard* has arrived with coal from the northeast and waits to be unloaded next day, while 4-6-0 No 5059 *Earl St Aldwyn* is shunting the carriage sidings.

Right: On 6 February 1960 the driver of 4-6-0 No 5050 *Earl of St Germans* awaits the 'right away' from Newton Abbot on his 216-mile journey home to Shrewsbury with the 8am from Plymouth to Liverpool and Glasgow, now with the Kingswear to Manchester coaches attached.

All photographs were taken by the author.

Ian Allan
PUBLISHING

First published 1999

ISBN 0 7110 2648 3

© Peter W. Gray 1999

Published by Ian Allan Publishing

An imprint of Ian Allan Publishing Ltd, Terminal House, Shepperton, Surrey TW17 8AS.
Printed by Ian Allan Printing Ltd, Riverdene Business Park, Hersham, Surrey KT12 4RG.

Code: 9904/C2

Introduction

The early history of the West of England main lines saw the broad gauge companies supported the Great Western Railway able to proceed apace through Somerset and Devon, while their rival the narrow gauge London & South Western Railway had been unable to proceed beyond Dorchester, along its then expected more southerly route to the west.

By 1849 the main lines of the Bristol & Exeter and South Devon railways were complete and the broad gauge had reached Plymouth. But bridging the River Tamar was to take another 10 years, partly because raising the capital for railway building became more difficult, the further west the railway penetrated into the then impoverished countryside.

Meanwhile, the LSWR's progress westwards was still held at Dorchester, despite various proposals for lines to Exeter. The next local development was the takeover by the GWR of the Wilts, Somerset & Weymouth Railway, which had been making very slow progress southwards and was then only open to Westbury. This line through Yeovil and Dorchester to Weymouth was completed by the GWR in January 1857.

The passage of the Salisbury & Yeovil Railway Bill in 1854 determined that the LSWR's future progress westwards would now be by that route and with the LSWR itself building the extension to Exeter concurrently, the whole line was open to Exeter Queen Street by July 1860.

Despite its earlier lack of progress westwards, the LSWR had signalled its intention by the illegal purchase in 1847 of Cornwall's first locomotive-hauled line, the Bodmin & Wadebridge Railway, and by acquiring a controlling interest in what became the North Devon line to Barnstaple. This line opened from Exeter St David's to Crediton in May 1851, as a broad gauge line leased to the Bristol & Exeter Railway, with the extension to Barnstaple following in August 1854, still on the broad gauge. However, by 1863, with the link line down from Exeter Queen Street to St David's completed, the main line to Barnstaple was now a single mixed gauge track leased to the LSWR.

By May 1859 the Royal Albert Bridge at Saltash was complete and it was possible to open the Cornwall Railway throughout to Truro, where it made an end-on junction with the West Cornwall Railway, opened in 1852 from Penzance to Truro on the narrow gauge and on which mixed gauge was laid by 1866.

Although the LSWR had agreed in 1862 not to proceed west beyond Okehampton, its sights were still set on Plymouth and Padstow. Initially as the Devon & Cornwall Railway, the narrow gauge line reached Okehampton in 1871, Lydford in 1874 and then via mixed gauge on the GWR's Launceston branch, through Plymouth to Devonport in May 1876. Towards the north coast of Cornwall, the line from Meldon Junction to Halwill opened through to Holsworthy in January 1879. It took another LSWR subsidiary, the North Cornwall Railway, to reach Launceston in 1886 and the LSWR finally opened its Padstow terminus in March 1899.

Meanwhile, the independent Plymouth, Devonport & South Western Junction Railway had completed the LSWR's main line into Plymouth, from Lydford to Devonport, by June 1890 and LSWR trains finally reached the new terminus at Friary in 1891.

The pattern of main lines in the southwest peninsular was now complete.

In this book, which is complementary to my earlier *Steam on West Country Branch Lines*, I have attempted to show the main lines west of Bristol/Weymouth as they were during the closing years of the steam railway using slides taken between 1957 and 1965.

We start from Bristol Temple Meads towards Taunton, before diverging to the Yeovil-Weymouth line, and then picking up the old LSWR route from Yeovil Junction through Exeter to the North Devon line. The GWR main line is then followed from Taunton to Penzance, with a couple of views on the Newquay branch justified by its status as a 'main line' on summer Saturdays, when it despatched eight express trains, only two less than the number starting from Penzance.

In the concluding pages we return to the LSWR route, tracing the North Cornwall line back to Okehampton, and then down to Plymouth, before finishing with the other 'main line' branch, the Kingswear line, which on peak 1958 summer Saturdays was sending out 37 trains, while in total only 27 came up from Plymouth and Cornwall.

For those interested in the technical details, the early pictures up to the spring of 1959 were taken with a folding 35mm Voigtlander Vito IIa camera with a f3.5 Color-Skopar lens. This was replaced by a new Agfa Super Silette fixed lens camera equipped with a f2 Solagon lens, while by summer 1965 I was using a Pentax S1a. The reproduction is with one exception from original slides, almost all either Kodachrome I or II, the others being Agfa CT18.

Lastly, I should like to thank those friends who have assisted by supplying information to enhance the caption details, amongst whom I should name Derek Frost, Alastair Jeffery, Richard Woodley and Eric Youldon. I do hope that you will enjoy this selection of views of our West of England main lines.

Peter W. Gray
Torquay
September 1998

With an insignificant load for this powerful locomotive, 'Merchant Navy' class 4-6-2 No 35006 *Peninsular & Oriental S.N. Co*, then only recently rebuilt from its original 'air-smoothed' form, climbs Honiton Incline near Wilmington on 18 June 1960 with coaches from the 1pm Waterloo, forming the 3.41pm stopping service from Templecombe to Exeter Central.

Above: When Laira's spotless 4-6-0 No 4087 *Cardigan Castle* pulled out of Bristol Temple Meads with the Sunday 1.30pm service to Plymouth on 25 March 1962, the station layout was substantially as it had been rebuilt by the Great Western Railway in 1935. The curved trainshed, which is still the heart of the station today, had been built during the 1870s as an addition to the original GWR terminus designed by Brunel, and to replace the Bristol & Exeter Railway's 'cow shed' which formerly stood on the area beyond the diesel shunter to be seen through No 4087's exhaust.

Right: 4-6-0 No 6914 *Langton Hall* is running into Yatton with the 12.6pm (Saturdays only) service from Bristol Temple Meads to Taunton on 4 March 1961. This train had an 11min layover at Weston-super-Mare, while it was overtaken by the down 'Cornishman' express from Wolverhampton to Penzance.

Left: Only on the Southern Region were the BR Standard Class 5 4-6-0s given names, where they took up some of the names of the 'King Arthur' class 4-6-0s they had deposed. No 73080 *Merlin* is pictured soon after leaving Yeovil (Pen Mill) station with the 1.5pm from Bristol Temple Meads to Weymouth on 18 July 1964, as it approaches the overbridge carrying the Salisbury to Exeter main line.

Above: The guard having advised the pilot engine driver of the train details, the 1.30pm to Waterloo is now ready to leave Weymouth behind BR Standard Class 4 2-6-0 No 76031 and rebuilt 'Battle of Britain' class Pacific No 34071 *601 Squadron* on 14 August 1965.

Above: The four-mile slog out of Weymouth eases imperceptibly from 1 in 50 to 1 in 52 passing the site of Upwey Wishing Well Halt, which had already been closed for over eight years as the 1.30pm from Weymouth to Waterloo passed by on 17 July 1965 behind a pair of BR Standard Class 5 4-6-0s. The leading engine, No 73083, appears to have lost its allocated name *Pendragon*, while the train engine, No 73029, has the earlier style of BR1 tender.

Right: The heavy second Boat Train out of Weymouth Quay on Saturday 17 July 1965 is assisted into Bincombe tunnel by rebuilt Bulleid 'Merchant Navy' class Pacific No 35017 *Belgian Marine*, with sister engine No 35005 *Canadian Pacific* at its head, now well into the tunnel and still on the 1 in 52 gradient.

Left: For trains heading westwards, Yeovil Junction lies at the foot of a succession of mainly downward gradients, so the Surbiton-Okehampton Car Carrier train is speeding past on the through road behind rebuilt 'Merchant Navy' class 4-6-2 No 35019 *French Line C.G.T.* on 18 July 1964.

Under the up side bracket signal stands BR Standard Class 5 4-6-0 No 73161 with the 8.47am from Exeter Central to Templecombe. This engine later returned to Yeovil Junction 'light engine' and subsequently worked the 12.6pm service to Salisbury.

The shuttle service to Yeovil Town, which is also signalled away, was by now powered by an ex-GWR 0-6-0 pannier tank, No 6435, and two auto trailers.

Above: Similarly, up express trains pass through Seaton Junction at high speed after racing down Honiton Incline, as well demonstrated here by rebuilt 'Merchant Navy' class Pacific No 35029 *Ellerman Lines* on the 4.30pm from Exeter Central to Waterloo. With a relief train running ahead of it on Whit Monday 11 June 1962, this train now conveys only the Torrington and Ilfracombe portions, plus restaurant car and extra coaches from Exeter.

In the up sidings Maunsell 'S15' class 4-6-0 No 30823 is ready to follow with the 5.18pm milk and parcels train from Sidmouth Junction to Waterloo.

Left: With no booked stop at Seaton Junction, 'Battle of Britain' class Pacific No 34086 *219 Squadron* was able to tackle the 1 in 80 Incline to Honiton Tunnel at speed with the through Brighton-Plymouth Buffet Express on 3 August 1964.

Above: Rebuilt 'Merchant Navy' c lass Pacific No 35006 *Peninsular & Oriental S.N. Co* is also making good progress a little further up the bank, passing the ground level Honiton Incline signal box about a mile before the tunnel mouth with 1pm Waterloo to Plymouth express, also on 3 August 1964.

Above: Snow, which had fallen soon after Christmas, is still evident on the north facing slopes above Honiton Tunnel, as the record breaking ex-LNER 'A4' class Pacific No 60022 *Mallard* emerges with the 'Westcountryman Rail Tour', organised by the Locomotive Club of Great Britain, on 24 February 1963. This tour later traversed the Exe Valley line and Tiverton branch, while *Mallard* was being serviced.

Participants also travelled over the Hemyock branch, before returning to London behind *Mallard* from Tiverton Junction.

Right: While there was evidence of the down side awning having been extended at Sidmouth Junction, there was precious little cover for passengers joining the up trains on wet days. As another shower commences, passengers hasten to join the 1.10pm from Exeter Central to Salisbury, hauled by 'West Country' class Pacific No 34015 *Exmouth* on 2 November 1963. In the down side bay platform is the connecting 1.45pm to Sidmouth, headed by BR Standard Class 3 2-6-2T No 82001, which will itself connect at Tipton St Johns with the 2pm departure to Exmouth via Budleigh Salterton.

Left and above: On 3 October 1963 rebuilt 'Merchant Navy' class 4-6-2 No 35010 *Blue Star* pulls confidently away from Exeter Central station with the up 'Atlantic Coast Express', by now down to two portions from Padstow and Ilfracombe only.

It had been a different scene when I first encountered these fine machines at Exeter Central back in 1942, Southern Railway No 21C10 then painted black and not named until December 1942. Some drivers, more accustomed to the sure-footed 'King Arthur' class 4-6-0s, had not yet adjusted their technique to suit the new Pacifics, and some awesome slipping occurred as they attempted to start the heavy wartime Waterloo bound trains out of Exeter Central. In the above picture 'West Country' class 4-6-2 No 34030 *Watersmeet* is probably being prepared to take over the following Plymouth-Brighton express.

Left: The approach to Exeter Central station from the west, up the steep 1 in 37 gradient from Exeter St David's station, had for many years needed the use of four engines to lift the heaviest of the Meldon ballast trains to the summit. However, the last years of steam operation saw another traffic which needed four engines, the Saturday block cement train from Westbury to Exeter Central.

The severity of the gradient is obvious here as BR Standard Class 4 2-6-4T No 80059 and ex-GWR 4-6-0 No 6963 *Throwley Hall*, assisted in the rear by ex-SR 'W' class 2-6-4Ts Nos 31911 and 31914, bring the Westbury cement train under Queen Street and into Central station on 28 September 1963.

Above: Ex-LSWR 'T9' class 4-4-0 No 30726 drops down the bank from Exeter Central station into St David's with the 3.48pm from Exeter Central to Okehampton on 4 April 1959.

Standing in the junction between the Southern and Western Region main lines is Exeter West signalbox, soon to be repainted in cream and chocolate, but at the time sadly in need of some attention. This box is now preserved, and operational on high days and holidays, at the Crewe Heritage Centre.

Above: The Southern main lines to Barnstaple Junction and Okehampton parted company at Coleford Junction, which is off picture to the right. In the background the line to north Devon can be seen, while in the foreground, passing a typical Southern lattice signal post with co-acting arms, in a lucky patch of sunlight, is BR Standard Class 5 4-6-0 No 73162 with the Plymouth portion of the 9am from Waterloo on 20 June 1964.

Right: Despite being the main line to north Devon, some 18 miles, from Copplestone to Umberleigh, was single track. It is on this section that 'Battle of Britain' class 4-6-2 No 34069 *Hawkinge* is passing Colleton Mills, south of Kings Nympton, with the 2.20pm from Ilfracombe to Waterloo, the rear portion of the 4.30pm from Exeter Central, on 23 August 1963.

Above: Forty Steps bridge was a favourite haunt of Taunton observers, giving a panoramic view of the western approach to Taunton station. It is Saturday 11 August 1962, by which time most of the main line passenger workings west of Taunton were diesel-hauled, and some steam engines were being put into temporary storage. 2-6-2Ts Nos 4593 and 5554 are in the sidings below with two pannier tanks. On the down

main line 4-6-0 No 7030 *Cranbrook Castle* is steaming through with the 11.5am from Paddington to Paignton at 1.52pm, 16min late. The steam arising from the station is coming from 2-6-2T No 6155 on the down relief line, which is about to leave Taunton for Minehead with the 10.15am from Paddington, which had arrived behind 4-6-0 No 4904 *Binnegar Hall* at 1.47pm.

Right: Looking west from the same viewpoint a little earlier that afternoon, 4-6-0 No 5092 *Tresco Abbey* is running through under clear signals at 1.17pm, probably on the Perranporth and Falmouth to Paddington train. In the carriage sidings beyond, 2-6-2T No 5563 stands with the stock for the 2pm departure for Yeovil (Pen Mill), having arrived at Taunton from Yeovil at 12.50pm.

Left: Recently still working not far away, on the West Somerset Railway, 4-6-0 No 4920 *Dumbleton Hall,* then based at Taunton shed, was on 26 July 1958 labouring up the final 1 in 80 stretch to the mouth of Whiteball tunnel, with the 12 coaches of the Saturday 9.40am from Paddington to Paignton.

Above: Nearly three years later, 4-6-0 No 7903 *Foremarke Hall* pounds out of the tunnel to the summit outside Whiteball Siding signalbox with the Saturday 7.30am service from Paddington to Kingswear on 1 July 1961. Note that on both embankments the long grass has been cut back, but controlled burning has still to be carried out on the up side.

25

Above: Looking over the bridge at Burlescombe today, it is difficult to realise there was once a station here. But it was still open on 1 July 1961 as 4-6-0 No 4904 *Binnegar Hall* drifted down towards Tiverton Junction, where it would pick up the milk tanks from Hemyock and form the 5pm Tiverton Junction to West Ealing milk train.

Right: The relative peace of Tiverton Junction station is shattered for a few moments on 1 June 1963 as 2-8-0 No 2882 races through with the Westbury-Exeter Central cement train, while a 'Warship' class diesel-hydraulic murmurs at the head of an up mixed freight.

Above: Not all the trains on the main lines were hauled by big engines, and although 'smalls' goods traffic to local stations had been concentrated on area depots for road distribution, there was still plenty of wagon load traffic into the early 1960s. 2-6-2T No 5560 is propelling a long rake of empties into the up refuge siding at Silverton on 9 December 1961, alongside the staggered down platform.

Right: The weekday 'Torbay Express' went over to diesel-hydraulic haulage in July 1959, but 4-6-0 No 5950 *Wardley Hall* was substituting as the up train passed Cowley Bridge on 12 March 1960.

Above: The last few Saturdays of the winter timetable were always an interesting period, because an increasing number of holiday relief trains were super-imposed upon the normal winter service. At Exeter St David's station at 2.8pm on 11 June 1960, we have the unusual sight of one relief train overtaking another, but not as would normally be the case with the non-stop train using the up main line, because this is occupied by the stationary 12.35pm from Paignton to Birmingham, hauled by BR Standard '9F' class 2-10-0 No 92204. Instead, the non-stop relief to the up 'Cornish Riviera Express', headed by 4-6-0 No 6016 *King Edward V*, has been forced to wend its way slowly around platform No 6 before regaining the main line.

Right: After the severe flooding which had occurred in the Exe, Culm and Creedy valleys during the preceding weeks, it was no surprise to learn that, due to a collapsed culvert near Burlescombe, all the down trains were running very late on 29 October 1960. A special relief train had been laid on at short notice to fill the gap in the service, giving rise to the unusual sight of Exeter's 2-6-0 No 7316 departing for Plymouth from platform No 1 under express headlamp code.

Left: Summer Sunday mornings in 1959 saw the departure from Paddington of three expresses to Plymouth and Cornwall during half an hour. This is the last of the batch, the 11.0am to Plymouth on 28 June, passing Starcross station behind 4-6-0 No 6002 *King William IV.* Although Starcross station is still open today, the up side buildings shown here no longer exist because, as Peter Kay says in his history of the Exeter to Newton Abbot line, when they were demolished in 1981, 'Nobody seems ever to have noticed that this was an 1846 Brunel station'.

Above: Well spruced up for its day trip to south Devon, ex-SR Class N 2-6-0 No 31875 is passing Cockwood harbour with a returning excursion train from Bere Alston to Goodrington Sands Halt on 16 June 1962.

Above: The view from Langstone Rock at 12.10pm on Tuesday 2 August 1960. 4-6-0 No 4975 *Umberslade Hall* is swinging around the curve, which takes the main line away from the Exe estuary and out onto the sea wall, with one of several empty stock trains scheduled to return stock to Paignton and Penzance after the Bank Holiday weekend. In the background sister engine No 5997 *Sparkford Hall* is running up 'light engine' and is almost under the old footbridge which marks the site of the original Warren Halt. Another up 'light engine' movement later that afternoon was 2-8-0T No 5264 returning to its home depot at Duffryn Yard, Port Talbot after a spell at St Blazey.

Right: The sea is not always in a friendly mood, and a south-easterly wind can soon whip up a swell that will swamp the down trains along the sea wall. 'Castle' class 4-6-0 No 4037 *The South Wales Borderers* is approaching Dawlish station with the 9.5am service from Liverpool to Plymouth on 17 September 1960, and the light patches on the coaches show where the sea has broken over them.

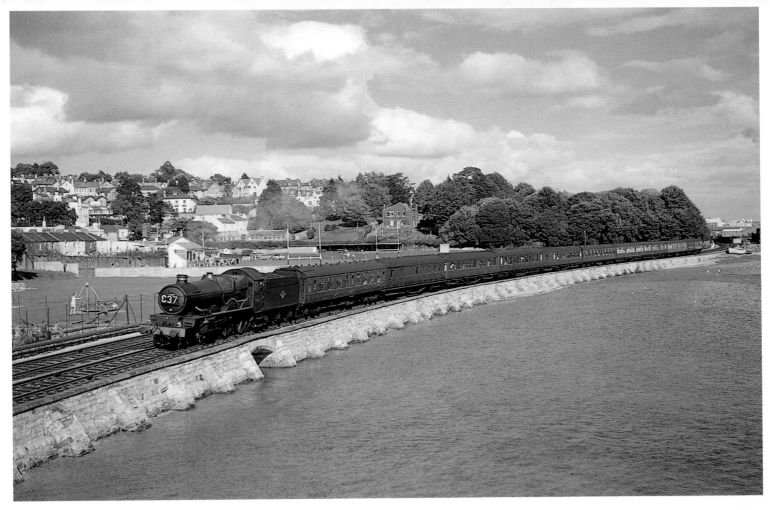

Left: Surprising as it might seem, many of the houses in Marine Parade (on the right of this picture) were constructed before the arrival of the South Devon Railway, which built the main line from Exeter to Plymouth. One can hardly imagine the furore that would be created if such a proposal were to be made today, but in 1846 the town was keen to have the railway and stipulated only that the line here should be low enough not to obstruct the views from the ground floor windows of the houses in Marine Parade.

On 27 August 1961 passers-by hardly notice the approach of 4-6-0 No 7014 *Caerhays Castle* as it breasts the rise into Dawlish station with the Sunday 4.10pm service from Paignton to Paddington. In the background, ahead of the engine, can be seen Coryton and Shell Coves and the approach to Parsons Tunnel.

Above: Children play on the swing, the rugby football goal posts are up and a match appears to be in progress; autumn is approaching on this penultimate Saturday of the summer service as the 12.20pm service from Cardiff to Newquay skirts the blue waters of the river Teign at Shaldon bridge behind 'Castle' class 4-6-0 No 5058 *Earl of Clancarty* on 3 September 1960.

37

Left: Farther up the Teign estuary, passing Hackney's Outer Home signal, 2-6-2T No 4150 is coasting towards Newton Abbot with the 5.44pm stopper from Exeter St David's on 18 August 1959.

Above: A feature of the traditional 1950s summer Saturday timetable at Newton Abbot was the disproportionate number of non-stop trains on the up relief road, coming off the Kingswear branch, when compared with the down side, where only two passenger trains were not booked to stop — all day. In 1961 the first of the up non-stops was the 6.50am from Paignton to Bradford, being hastened through by 4-6-0 No 5953 *Dunley Hall* on 29 July 1961.

Left: One is tempted to ask, 'How many dust-coated Post Office men does it take to unload Royal Mail Sorting Carriage No W799W?'. But no doubt by the time the mail sacks are five deep on the barrow, it will take all of them to shift it. This scene is being enacted at the west end of Newton Abbot's platform No 4 as 4-6-0 No 5934 *Kneller Hall* waits for pilot engine 4-6-0 No 7813 *Freshford Manor* to attach, before leaving for Penzance with the 11.30pm (Friday) from Liverpool (Lime Street) on Saturday 29 August 1959.

Above: The west end of Newton Abbot station as seen from the road, looking across to the locomotive shed, with the Locomotive Factory beyond it, far left. The vehicles on the right are standing outside the Carriage and Wagon Works with the houses of Forde Road behind.

Outside the shed the recently completed, and much needed, new shed office building stands out, a product of the 1955 Modernisation Plan, as is the skeleton of the new DMU inspection building on the far left, alongside the coaling plant, itself soon to be demolished.

It is 6.10pm on Wednesday 22 July 1959 and 4-6-0

No 1016 *County of Hants* has just arrived 'on time' from Shrewsbury with the 10.45am Manchester (London Rd) to Plymouth and Kingswear train, which will split here. 2-6-2T No 4174 has only just backed on to the 5.15pm down stopper from Exeter St David's to take it down to Paignton. The engine which brought this train in is now taking water (behind the Manchester's first coach) and will then take the rear portion down to Kingswear. 'Battle of Britain' class 4-6-2 No 34081 *92 Squadron* is between turns on the 'exchange' working, of which there are more details overleaf.

Left: The 'exchange' workings commenced early in the Second World War as a means of maintaining drivers' route knowledge in case diversions became necessary because of enemy action. The regular engines then working over the GWR route between Exeter and Plymouth were the Southern Railway 'N' class 2-6-0s on up to three daily workings, two passenger and one goods. The goods workings ceased after the war ended and gradually the 'West Country' class Pacifics took over until in the 1950s the 'Ns' were rarely seen,

although a 'U' class Mogul was used on one occasion.

By the summer of 1959, the previous regular workings between Exeter and Plymouth had been disrupted by closure of the wayside stations between Brent and Plymouth and by the arrival of the diesel-hydraulics. Consequently, the up afternoon working was now on the 4.35pm from Plymouth to Paignton, as far as Newton Abbot, where the engine was turned and waited for the 7.20pm from Goodrington Sands Halt to Plymouth, which 'Battle of Britain' class 4-6-2

No 34063 *229 Squadron* is here accelerating away from Aller Junction on 17 June 1959.

Above: Consecutively numbered engines double-heading is something of a rarity, but rolling down towards the Aller Junction up distant signal, with Stoneycombe Quarry in the background, are 'Castle' class 4-6-0s Nos 5066 *Sir Felix Pole* and 5065 *Newport Castle* with the 7.30am from Penzance to Wolverhampton on Saturday 3 September 1960.

43

Left: In the classic evening location, on the steepest part of Dainton bank, two engines approach the tunnel with the 10.29am from Manchester (Exchange) on 21 July 1960. The train engine, looking in ex-Works condition, is 4-6-0 No 7916 *Mobberley Hall*, for several years a Newton Abbot engine, but then recently transferred to Laira, while the more careworn pilot is 2-6-2T No 5153, one of Newton Abbot's large fleet of '5101' class engines.

Above: At the signalbox end of Dainton Tunnel, 4-6-0 No 7018 *Drysllwyn Castle* is about to complete the stiff climb from Totnes with the 1.10pm from Plymouth to Liverpool on 13 April 1957. *Drysllwyn Castle* was then still attached to the Western Region self-weighing tender, which had been used for test runs since the fitting of a new double-chimney. This was frame No 17 of my first colour transparency film, exposed at 1/125th of a second at f3.5 on Kodachrome I.

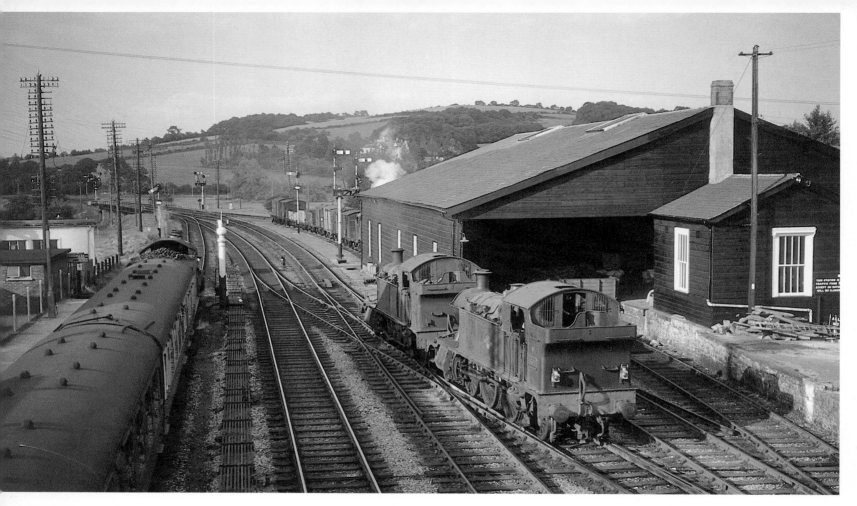

Above: The substantial black goods shed was a prominent feature of Totnes station, until it burnt down one day, hopefully not set alight by a spark from one of the Totnes bankers, which often snoozed inside between turns. On this evening, 29 June 1960, a '5101' class banker is out in the open beyond the goods shed as 2-6-2Ts Nos 4555 and 4561 run around the returning Buckfastleigh Combined Sunday Schools excursion train, which is on its way back from Teignmouth. While the children had been on the beach, the stock had spent the day in the sidings at Exminster. In the up platform a Newton Abbot 'Castle' class 4-6-0 heads the 6.5pm from Plymouth to Newton Abbot.

Right: Climbing out of Totnes the gradient is mainly in the 1 in 50s, but just beyond Tigley signalbox it eases to the 70s and then to the 90s, as mixed-traffic 2-8-0 No 4706 brings the Sunday 4.15pm Exeter-Plymouth stopping service past the box on 30 August 1959. This service was a convenient way of returning to Laira the '47XX' class engine which had worked down from London the previous day on the 1.25pm from Paddington to Kingswear, and subsequently returned to Exeter during the Saturday evening on a local train. No 4706 is in the externally neglected condition typical of many Bristol St Philip's Marsh engines at that time.

Left: Still on gently rising gradients to the South Devon main line summit at Wrangaton, where the station had been closed earlier in 1959, on 20 June that year 4-6-0 No 6911 *Holker Hall* is piloting North British Locomotive Co Type 4 diesel-hydraulic No D601 *Ark Royal* on the Saturday 11.5am from Paddington to Penzance.

Steam piloting of the early 'Warship' class diesel-hydraulics was quite common during 1959, when they were limited to a 10-coach load over the South Devon banks, remembering that by this date only four of the prototype NBL Type 2 'D63XX' diesel-hydraulic locomotives, later to be used as pilot engines, had as yet been delivered.

Since passing through Brent station, with Brent Hill in the background, the train has swept round a more than 90 degree curve and is now hugging the edge of Dartmoor, close to the 450ft contour, and approaching Glazebrook Viaduct.

Above: Ivybridge station was located on a sharp curve at the west end of Ivybridge Viaduct, a double track brick structure which replaced Brunel's single track broad gauge viaduct in 1893. The Brunel station building on the left, set well back from the main line, was originally close to the broad gauge line, whose viaduct lay to the north (left) of the 1893 replacement. Passing through the station on 14 June 1958 are 4-6-0s No 5075 *Wellington* ('Castle' class) and No 6915 *Mursley Hall* with the Saturday 12.5pm from Paddington to Plymouth.

Left: Plymouth's Laira depot was opened in 1906, when the GWR outgrew its original facilities at Millbay. At first a single roundhouse sufficed, but in 1932 a straight shed was added alongside. This can be seen on the left, with the roundhouse hidden behind it, beyond which is the main line.

The foreground tracks between Lipson Junction (on the main line) and Mount Gould Junction were opened in 1891 to allow LSWR trains to reach their new terminus at Friary.

The locomotives leaving the depot via the shed exit road on 2 May 1959 are 4-6-0s Nos 5999 *Wollaton Hall* and 6016 *King Edward V*. They will reverse back over the crossover, through Lipson Junction and down to Plymouth station, to await the arrival of the 12 noon from Penzance, which they will then work forward to Newton Abbot.

Above: In the summer of 1961 the new Plymouth station office block was still under construction and the platforms next to the concourse were still through roads. Nowadays the Gunnislake trains leave from the left hand track, where 4-6-0 No 6814 *Enborne Grange* stands on 17 June 1961 with the 12.5pm to Redruth. Beside it are ex-LSWR 'M7' class 0-4-4 tanks Nos 30036 and 30034 on eight coaches forming the 12.18pm to Tavistock North.

51

Above: There is something to be said for the road bridge between St Budeaux and Saltash — it makes a good platform from which to photograph Brunel's masterpiece of 1859, as 4-6-0 No 7022 *Hereford Castle* brings the relief to the 4.50pm from Penzance to Manchester across in subdued evening light on 4 August 1962.

Right: 0-6-0PT No 6419 propels the 6.42pm Plymouth auto across Forder Viaduct towards St Germans on the evening of 31 July 1959. Above the leading auto trailer can be seen a stone bridge which once spanned what had been the old Cornwall Railway main line, still in use as a siding in 1959, before the present double track line was built farther inland by the GWR. Redundant Royal Navy ships are moored in the Hamoaze beyond.

52

Left: By 1961 steam workings on the main line through Cornwall were quite limited, so to manage to get two in one picture was very lucky indeed. Heading away from the camera across Nottar Viaduct over the Lynher river is 4-6-0 No 6988 *Swithland Hall* on the 1pm from Plymouth to Penzance, while 4-6-0 No 1004 *County of Somerset* is taking the 10.45am from Penzance to Plymouth towards Shillingham Tunnel on August Bank Holiday Monday 7 August 1961.

Above: Rush hour at Liskeard! 2-6-2T No 5532 arrived hauling the 5.35pm Plymouth-Liskeard auto at 6.25pm and has now shunted across to the up line, clear of 4-6-0 No 5058 *Earl of Clancarty* which was following with the 12.20pm Cardiff to Newquay service on Saturday 15 July 1961.

Above: Although not the highest, standing 147ft above the East Looe river, Moorswater viaduct is surely the most spectacular of all the many viaducts on the Cornish main line. Crossing it with the up 'Cornish Riviera Express' on 15 August 1959 is 'Castle' class 4-6-0 No 5066 *Sir Felix Pole.* On the left can be seen four of the piers of Brunel's original timber viaduct, replaced by the present structure in 1881.

Right: When it came to rebuilding Largin viaduct in the Glynn valley, the original piers were used and the ingenious GWR engineers managed to do this without significantly holding up traffic on the line while the work was being done. When 4-6-0 No 5972 *Olton Hall* brought the 7.20am from Truro to Plymouth across Largin Viaduct on 19 July 1958 it was still double track, but this section was later singled in 1964.

Left: From high on the hill looking down on Clinnick Viaduct, one of the early ones to be rebuilt, in 1879, the beautiful wooded slopes of the Glynn valley can best be appreciated. From this position one also gets the full effect of the 'stack music' as 4-6-0 No 1007 *County of Brecknock* tackles the 1 in 68 climb with the 12 multi-coloured coaches, including a Dining Car, of the 8.35am from Falmouth to Paddington on Saturday 8 August 1959.

Above: 4-6-0 No 4906 *Bradfield Hall* was one of St Blazey shed's small complement of main line engines, here seen charging through Bodmin Road station with the 8.5am from Newquay to Sheffield and Newcastle at 9.23am on Saturday 4 July 1959.

Standing on the down road in the station is 4-6-0 No 7925 *Westol Hall*, at that time Penzance's only Modified Hall, on the 7.55am Plymouth to Penzance parcels and empty milk tanks.

A few minutes earlier 2-6-2T No 5557 had left with the 9.15am service to Bodmin General, after connecting with the 11.50pm overnight sleeper train from Paddington hauled by 4-6-0 No 4950 *Patshull Hall*.

Above: Running non-stop from St Austell to Bodmin Road, the 10.45am from Penzance to Sheffield is racing through Par station on 2 July 1960, with the fireman building up a head of steam for the climb to come. Later, the driver of 4-6-0 No 4967 *Shirenewton Hall* will be faced with re-starting this 11-coach load from Bodmin Road on the long slog up the Glynn valley to Doublebois. There was some excitement at Par station later that afternoon, when 4-6-0 No 7929 *Wyke Hall* became derailed at the approach to the station from the Newquay line.

Right: When snow falls in Cornwall you have to catch it quickly, especially if the sun is out. On 3 March 1962 the 10.55am Plymouth-Penzance service, behind 4-6-0 No 6814 *Enborne Grange*, is approaching the spot beyond Burngullow, where some years later an old mineshaft was discovered right under the main line. Although now singled, the track is still heavily braced.

Above: The relieving crew at Truro have time to gossip with the men who have brought the 3.40pm Perishables train up from Penzance, before continuing towards Paddington aboard 4-6-0 No 1001 *County of Bucks* on 9 September 1961. Behind the engine is one of the Marazion restricted use express brake vans used on the broccoli specials and an ancient looking meat van, as an anonymous diesel shunter rumbles past.

Right: With Camborne still visible in the distance and the Carn Brea monument almost swallowed up in low cloud, 4-6-0 No 1006 *County of Cornwall* is approaching Gwinear Road East signalbox with the 3.40pm from Plymouth to Penzance on 12 July 1961.

Above: On alighting at St Erth from the overnight 11.50pm (Friday) Liverpool-Penzance train at 1.35pm on 14 July 1962, on which I had travelled from Newton Abbot behind NBL 'Warship' class diesel-hydraulic No D861 *Vigilant,* I recall being just ever so slightly miffed, that had I known that 4-6-0 No 1006 *County of Cornwall* was following 10min behind us on a Glasgow to Penzance relief train, I could have travelled the length of the Duchy behind steam that morning.

Right: The view from the wall above Penzance station on the same afternoon, looking around Mount's Bay towards Ponsandane sidings, Long Rock shed and Marazion. With the bad weather sheet extended, the driver of 4-6-0 No 1001 *County of Bucks* is slowly backing the stock for the 4.45pm relief to the 4.50pm to Manchester into the station. In the sidings is 4-6-0 No 6921 *Borwick Hall,* which had arrived at 3.25pm with a parcels train, which I took to be the late running 7.58am Plymouth parcels, due in at 1.5pm.

Above: On summer Saturdays anything from a 4-6-0 'Castle' to a 0-6-0 pannier tank, sometimes in combination, could be found working the passenger trains on the Newquay branch. On 19 July 1958, after crossing Goss moor from St Dennis Junction, and then climbing over the main A30 road, 2-6-0 No 6397 and 2-6-2T No 5539 are approaching the fixed distant at the summit of the line near Roche with the 12.40pm from Newquay to Cardiff. Upon reaching the main line at

Par, it is most likely that No. 5539 will be released, and No 6397 will continue alone to Plymouth.

The pattern of summer Saturday trains on the Newquay branch was strangely unbalanced, with eight full length trains leaving each Saturday up to 1.45pm for a range of destinations, but most incoming passengers, apart from those coming overnight or from Paddington, had to change at Par.

Right: Consequently, on Saturdays there was also a substantial service of local trains and two of these have crossed at Luxulyan on 8 July 1961. The steam from 4-6-0 No 6812 *Chesford Grange* can be seen in the distance, making for Bugle with the 12.25pm from Par to Newquay, while leaving for Par is 4-6-0 No 6875 *Hindford Grange* with the 11.52am from Newquay.

Above: The preservation in 'running order' of LSWR 'T9' class 4-4-0 No 120 was an opportunity too good to miss, when it came to planning the Railway Correspondence & Travel Society/Plymouth Railway Circle railtour for 1963. So it was that on 27 April 1963 No 120 ran from Exeter Central to Padstow and back, returning for one day to what had been a regular 'beat' for this class until the commencement of the 1961 summer timetable.

At Wadebridge the passengers are waiting to board the brake van special behind 0-6-0PT No 1369 (also now preserved) which ran to Wenford Bridge, while the 'T9' was being serviced at Wadebridge shed.

Right: The replacements for the 'T9s' on the North Cornwall line — after a short spell with 'U1' class 2-6-0s — were BR Standard Class 4 2-6-4Ts. No 80041 is approaching Tresmeer with the 3.10pm from Padstow to Okehampton on 22 August 1964, which had been a regular 'T9' working through to Exeter Central. Although two-coach trains were not that uncommon latterly, the make-up of this one, with a maroon repainted Bulleid brake composite paired with an ex-LNER coach from the Thompson period, is unusual.

Left: The sense of urgency felt on the Southern, when trains were running late, can be detected here at Halwill Junction, or Halwill for Beaworthy according to the running in board, caught at a busy moment on Tuesday 4 August 1964, at around 6.30pm. The delayed 5.51pm from Okehampton to Wadebridge, (see page 72) whose engineless coaches are standing on the right, is being further delayed while the train engine, 'U' class 2-6-0

No 31802, fetches three more coaches from the yard to attach to the front of the train.

Meanwhile, the platform staff are hastening the despatch of the 6.25pm to Bude, which already has the road from the bay platform, and in the background the 6.30pm to Torrington is departing from its separate bay platform on the up side.

Above: It was much more peaceful at Halwill Junction at 6.5pm on Saturday 22 August 1964. The gates are open to allow 'N' class 2-6-0 No 31845 to leave for Ashbury with the lightly loaded Bude goods. The black object in the distance is Ivatt 2-6-2T No 41249 arriving with the 4.40pm from Torrington.

Above: The delay to the 5.51pm from Okehampton to Wadebridge on Tuesday 4 August 1964 had been caused by the long wait it had at Ashbury, the previous crossing station, while 'N' class 2-6-0 No 31846 on the Bude goods, on this day with a trailing load which must have been close to the maximum, toiled slowly up the 1 in 78 through the station, every exhaust beat echoing back from the distant Dartmoor hills. In just over a month's time all freight services were to be withdrawn from the North Cornwall line.

Right: Still earlier that day, 4 August 1964, 'U' class 2-6-0 No 31802 is seen near East Bowerland, between Maddaford Moor Halt and Meldon Junction, with the 1.0pm from Padstow to Okehampton. Evidence of the transfer of these Southern lines to the Western Region is well to the fore in this train.

Above: At Okehampton the porter pauses before mounting the steps in front of the signalbox to clean one of the station signs, while in platform No 1 BR Standard Class 4 2-6-4T No 80042 prepares to depart with the 1.30pm to Bude. In the background, 'N' class 2-6-0 No 31406 has backed a short ballast train into the military sidings and waits for Ivatt 2-6-2T No 41317 to back on as pilot engine, before leaving for Exeter on 4 August 1964.

Right: Between Lydford and Tavistock the ex-Southern main line to Plymouth used the same valley as the earlier ex-GWR branch line to Launceston. With Brentor in the background and Brentor station on the Southern line just around the corner behind the hill, 'Battle of Britain' class 4-6-2 No 34081 *92 Squadron* takes the Plymouth portion of the 8.35am from Waterloo towards Tavistock North on 4 August 1962.

Above: Although I appreciate that anyone who has lived near a busy marshalling yard may have other views, on a peaceful summer's afternoon the sound of a steam engine shunting loose-coupled wagons; a few puffs followed by the 'ching, ching, ching' of many pairs of buffers as the wagons close up on each other, can be very restful. This was the scene at Bere Alston on 24 June 1961 as 'N' class 2-6-0 No 31849 shunted the yard on the up side. In the distant background is Kit Hill on the Cornish side of the Tamar valley, which lies hidden below. *Peter W. Gray / Colour Rail*

Right: On 29 September 1959 the entry into Plymouth station from the east was still dominated by this semaphore gantry, under which 'West Country' class 4-6-2 No 34023 *Blackmore Vale* is taking the empty stock of the 11.47am Exeter Central-Plymouth service round to Friary, although Friary station had then been closed for 12 months.

This area, almost alongside the Eye Infirmary, had been until 1939 the site of Mutley station, which was closed to allow the rebuilding of Plymouth North Road station to proceed. This project was however halted by the war and not eventually completed until 1962.

Above: It was the replacement of Hoodown Viaduct outside Kingswear in 1928, that allowed the GWR's heaviest locomotives to work over the whole of the Kingswear branch, and thereafter 'King' class 4-6-0s regularly worked the 'Torbay Express' until 1948. By 1960 they were seen less frequently, but on Whit Sunday 5 June 1960 No 6021 *King Richard II* worked the 10.40am from Paddington to Kingswear, and is seen here at Paignton station on Tuesday 7 June preparing to return to London on the 4.25pm relief from Paignton to Paddington.

Right: Beyond Goodrington Sands Halt the Kingswear branch has always been single track. Leaving the only crossing station at Churston, 4-6-0 No 5059 *Earl St Aldwyn* is passing Galmpton with the Kingswear portion of the 1.30pm from Paddington to Penzance the 'Royal Duchy' on 3 July 1961. Earlier in the day, this engine would have worked the 9.5am Liverpool to Plymouth express between Shrewsbury and Newton Abbot, where the leading coaches have been picked up from the yard to strengthen the four from London.